AN IRISH BLESSING

A PHOTOGRAPHIC INTERPRETATION BY CYRIL A. REILLY AND RENÉE TRAVIS REILLY

© 1999 by Cyril A. Reilly and Renée Travis Reilly

International Standard Book Number: 1-893732-01-0

Library of Congress Catalog Card Number: 99-61902

Cover and text design by Dwight Luna.

Printed and bound in the United States of America.

An Irish Blessing

A PHOTOGRAPHIC INTERPRETATION BY CYRIL A. REILLY AND RENÉE TRAVIS REILLY

SORIN BOOKS Notre Dame, Indiana

May the blessing of light be with you—
light outside and light within.

May sunlight shine upon you and warm your heart
'til it glows like a great peat fire
so that the stranger may come and warm himself by it,
and also a friend.

May a blessed light shine out of the two eyes of you
like a candle set in two windows of a house,
bidding the wanderer to come in out of the storm.

May the blessing of rain—the sweet, soft rain—fall upon your spirit
and wash it fair and clean.

May it leave many a shining pool where the blue of heaven shines,
and sometimes a star.

May the blessing of earth—the good, rich earth—be with you.

May you ever have a kindly greeting for those you pass
as you go along its roads.

May the earth be soft under you when you rest upon it,
tired at the end of the day.

May earth rest easy over you when at the last you lie under it.

May the earth rest so lightly over you
that your spirit may be out from under it quickly,
and up, and off, and on its way to God.

MAY THE BLESSING OF LIGHT BE WITH YOU—

Light outside and light within.

May sunlight shine upon you

AND WARM YOUR HEART

'TIL IT GLOWS LIKE A GREAT PEAT FIRE
SO THAT THE STRANGER MAY COME AND
WARM HIMSELF BY IT,

May a blessed light shine out of the two eyes of you

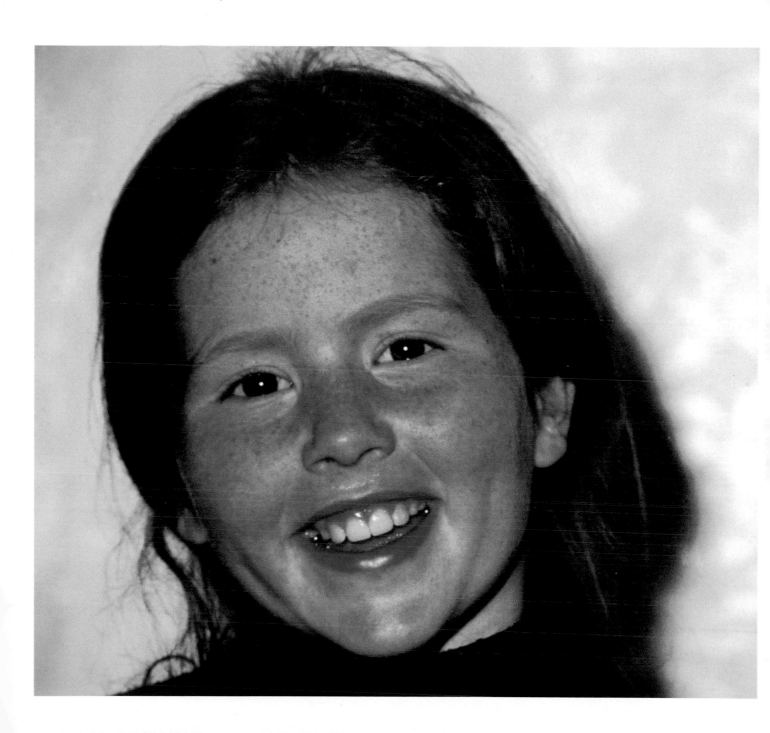

LIKE A CANDLE SET IN
TWO WINDOWS OF A HOUSE,

BIDDING THE WANDERER TO
COME IN OUT OF THE STORM.

MAY THE BLESSING OF RAIN—

THE SWEET, SOFT RAIN—FALL UPON YOUR SPIRIT AND WASH IT FAIR AND CLEAN.

May it leave many
a shining pool

WHERE THE BLUE OF HEAVEN SHINES,
AND SOMETIMES A STAR.

May the blessing of earth—

THE GOOD, RICH EARTH—BE WITH YOU.

MAY YOU EVER HAVE A KINDLY GREETING

FOR THOSE YOU PASS AS
YOU GO ALONG ITS ROADS.

May the earth be soft under you

WHEN YOU REST UPON IT,
TIRED AT THE END OF THE DAY.

May earth rest easy over you
when at the last you lie under it.

May the earth rest so lightly over you

That your spirit may be
out from under it quickly,

AND UP, AND OFF, AND ON ITS WAY TO GOD.